SHAMBHALA
CLASSICS

LAO TZU

TAO TEH CHING

TRANSLATED BY
JOHN C. H. WU

SHAMBHALA
BOSTON & LONDON
2005

Shambhala Publications, Inc.
Horticultural Hall
300 Massachusetts Avenue
Boston, Massachusetts 02115
www.shambhala.com

9 8 7 6 5 4 3 2 1

Printed in the United States of America
⊗ This edition is printed on acid-free paper that meets
the American National Standards Institute z39.48 Standard.
Distributed in the United States by Random House, Inc.,
and in Canada by Random House of Canada Ltd

The Library of Congress catalogues the previous edition
of this book as follows:

Lao-tzu.
[Tao te ching. English & Chinese]
Tao teh ching / Lao Tzu: translated by John C. H. Wu.
p.   cm.
Translation of: Tao te ching.
Reprint. Originally published: New York: St. John's
University, 1961.
(Asian Institute translations: no. 1).
ISBN 0-87773-388-0 (alk. paper)
ISBN 1-59030-246-x (Shambhala Classics)
I. Wu, Ching-hsuing, 1899–   II. Title.   III. Series: Asian
Institute translations: no. 1.
BL1900.L3E5   1989A
299'.51482—DC20
89-33467
CIP

TO

DR. SUN FO

CONTENTS

FOREWORD

A NEW ENGLISH TRANSLATION of the *Tao Teh Ching* is welcome, if it is faithful to the original, and lays hold of yet more of its great insights. These objectives Dr. John C. H. Wu has done his best to attain. He has carefully revised an earlier rendering which was published in the *T'ien Hsia Monthly* twenty years ago. In addition to competence in the Chinese language, Dr. Wu possesses two endowments necessary to a translator of this text: a practical understanding of men and institutions, and an appreciation of mysticism in its highest and best sense. In the 1920's he carried on an illuminating correspondence with the late Justice Oliver Wendell Homes—letters that were published in the aforementioned journal. It was natural that owing to his knowledge of comparative law he was chosen to write, in 1933, the *First Draft of the Permanent Constitution of China*. In 1946 there appeared, quite to the surprise of his friends, a translation of the *Book of Psalms* into the Chinese language.

It is vain to hope for a definitive English rendering of the *Tao Teh Ching*; and this expectation Dr. Wu would be among the first to disclaim. Any translation is an interpretation, particularly if the work is one of great imaginative insight; for the language of one tradition does not provide exact verbal equivalents for all the creative ideas of another tradition. The *Tao Teh Ching* is a series of insights into life and nature; it is suggestion rather than statement. Obliged as a translator is to choose a particular word, he is bound to leave other possibilities unexpressed; he cannot, as Chuang Tzu would say, play all the tunes at once. It does not follow, however, that one rendering cannot evoke more of the original music than another. An allied difficulty besetting a translator of this classic is worth mentioning: the obscurity of certain words and phrases, attributable it is believed to misplacement or loss of some of the wooden slips on which, before the invention of printing, the text was transmitted. Fortunately these instances are few, and may be ignored.

The *Tao Teh Ching* was written in the morning of the human race, and still bears the freshness of the morning upon it. It exhibits a rush of language, a boldness and exuberance of expression for which paradox is the only adequate form. Hence one who expects to find in it a reasoned, chain-like sequence of thought will be disappointed. Let him not, however, turn away from it on this account. For the Taoists, Reality was beyond measurement, but not beyond apprehension by a mind that is still. The Book's greatest gift, in my view, is its mind-stretching quality; it challenges us at every turn to expand our view of life's possibilities.

Both Confucianism and Taoism complement each other, however incompatible they seem at first sight to be. The former places a man in his proper relation to his fellow-men, the latter in proper relation to nature. A third philosophy, Buddhism, though introduced from India, deals with the problem of human suffering and with man's ultimate destiny. These three inheritances—the first adjusting man to his fellow-men, the second to nature, and the third to the Absolute—have moulded the thinking not only of the Chinese people but of all Eastern Asia. There is truth, then, in the common saying that every Chinese wears a Confucian cap, a Taoist robe, and Buddhist sandals.

Whereas Confucius counseled his people to labor untiringly for the welfare and dignity of man in society, Lao Tzu and Chuang Tzu on the other hand cautioned them against excessive interference. In their view, the urge to change what by nature is already good only increases the sum-total of human unhappiness. These two urges: on the one hand, to do something, and on the other hand, not to do too much, are forever contending in our natures. The man who can maintain a just balance between them is on the road to social and intellectual maturity.

Though Taoism by its nature is not a philosophy that could well be carried out in government, it nonetheless became the inspiration of much of Chinese literature and nearly all of Chinese art. It provided those "Waldens of the mind" that Dialectical Man needs to restore his sense of wonder and repose. Only the free, unfettered Taoist mind, bent on enjoying nature as well as conquering her, was able to engender in China a pure landscape art one thousand years before landscape art, for its own sake, made its appearance in Europe. Thanks to both Taoist and Zen influence, Japanese landscape art antedated that of Europe by six hundred years. Skill in the apportionment of space, economy of line and color, freedom and spontaneity in choice of subject and treatment, are all marks of Taoist thinking.

He who views with distrust excessive organization and mechanization, will find in the *Tao Teh Ching* man's first articulate protest against them. If he has misgivings about the notion of "inevitable progress," he is reminded by Lao Tzu that "all things come back to their roots," that "to go far is to return." The heavy blow, says Taoism, often fails where the light touch succeeds. The world has a place for humility, yielding, gentleness, and serenity. But to enjoy these benefits one must

"Learn to unlearn one's learning."

ARTHUR W. HUMMEL
Former Head, Division of Orientalia
Library of Congress, Washington, D.C.
1962

EDITOR'S NOTES

WITH regard to the author of *Tao Teh Ching*, there are various opinions. Some scholars hold that it was written by an elder contemporary of Confucius, Lao Tan, or more popularly called Lao Tzu, while others maintain that it was composed after Confucius, that is, sometime during the time of the Warring States. It is not possible at the present time to give any final judgment on this question of authorship. We can only be grateful to the author, whoever he was, for he has written one of the most profound works that has issued from the mind of man.

This translation is made from Wang Pi's edition 王弼 of the original text. The only points on which the translator has departed from Wang's reading are listed below:

1. In Chapter 10, Wang Pi has 天門開闔·能無雌乎·. The word 無 here is clearly a misprint for 為. Dr. Wu has followed what is generally considered the right reading. In this he is supported by many other editions.

2. In Chapter 15, the word 久 in 孰能安以久動之徐 生° is superfluous, and this translation has ignored it. Neither in the Ching Lung edition 景龍 nor in Wu Ch'en's 吳澄 is found the word 久.

3. In Chapter 15, Wang Pi has 儼兮其若容. In other editions the word 客 is used instead 容. The translator considers that 客 is the right reading.

4. In Chapter 20, Wang Pi has 如春登臺, while other editions have 如登春臺. This translation follows the latter.

5. In Chapter 29, Wang Pi has 或挫或隳. Both in Ho Shang Kung's edition 河上公 and in Wei Yuan's 魏源 the word 載 is used instead of 挫. As the translator considers that 載 is the right reading, he follows Ho's and Wei's editions.

6. In Chapter 34, the words 常無欲 are superfluous, and therefore they are not translated.

7. In Chapter 49, before 聖人皆孩之, some words are clearly missing. This translation follows Ho Shang Kung's edition by adding "All the people strain their ears and eyes." 百姓皆注其耳目.

The *Tao Teh Ching* consists of 81 chapters divided into two parts: the Upper Part and the Lower Part. The Upper Part, chapters 1 to 37, begins with the word "Tao" and is known as the *Tao Ching* (Classic of Tao). The Lower Part, chapters 38 to 81, begins with the words "Shang Teh" (High Virtue) and is known as the *Teh Ching* (Classic of Virtue). The *Tao Ching* and the *Teh Ching* constitute the complete work, the *Tao Teh Ching*.

PAUL K. T. SIH

TAO TEH CHING

一章

道可道非常道。名可名非常名。無名天地之始。有名萬物之母。故常無欲以觀其妙常有欲以觀其徼此兩者同出而異名。同謂之玄玄之又玄眾妙之門。

2

I

TAO can be talked about, but not the Eternal Tao.
Names can be named, but not the Eternal Name.

As the origin of heaven-and-earth, it is nameless:
As "the Mother" of all things, it is nameable.

So, as ever hidden, we should look at its inner essence:
As always manifest, we should look at its outer aspects.

These two flow from the same source, though differently
  named;
And both are called mysteries.

The Mystery of mysteries is the Door of all essence.

二章

天下皆知美之爲美，斯惡已，皆知善之爲善，斯不善已。

故有無相生，難易相成，長短相較，高下相傾，音聲相和，

前後相隨，是以聖人處無爲之事，行不言之教，萬物作

焉而不辭，生而不有，爲而不恃，功成而弗居，夫唯弗居，

是以不去。

2

WHEN all the world recognizes beauty as beauty,
　　this in itself is ugliness.
When all the world recognizes good as good, this in
　itself is evil.

Indeed, the hidden and the manifest give birth
　　to each other.
Difficult and easy complement each other.
Long and short exhibit each other.
High and low set measure to each other.
Voice and sound harmonize each other.
Back and front follow each other.

Therefore, the Sage manages his affairs without ado,
And spreads his teaching without talking.
He denies nothing to the teeming things.
He rears them, but lays no claim to them.
He does his work, but sets no store by it.
He accomplishes his task, but does not dwell upon it.

And yet it is just because he does not dwell on it
That nobody can ever take it away from him.

三章

不尚賢使民不爭。不貴難得之貨使民不爲盜不見可欲使民心不亂。是以聖人之治虛其心實其腹弱其志強其骨。常使民無知無欲。使夫知者不敢爲也爲無爲則無不治。

3

BY not exalting the talented you will cause the people to cease from rivalry and contention.

By not prizing goods hard to get, you will cause the people to cease from robbing and stealing.

By not displaying what is desirable, you will cause the people's hearts to remain undisturbed.

Therefore, the Sage's way of governing begins by

> Emptying the heart of desires,
> Filling the belly with food,
> Weakening the ambitions,
> Toughening the bones.

In this way he will cause the people to remain without knowledge and without desire, and prevent the knowing ones from any ado.

Practice Non-Ado, and everything will be in order.

四章

道冲而用之或不盈。淵兮似萬物之宗。挫其銳。解其紛。和其光。同其塵。湛兮似或存。吾不知誰之子。象帝之先。

4

THE Tao is like an empty bowl,
 Which in being used can never be filled up.
Fathomless, it seems to be the origin of all things.
It blunts all sharp edges,
It unties all tangles,
It harmonizes all lights,
It unites the world into one whole.
Hidden in the deeps,
Yet it seems to exist for ever.
I do not know whose child it is;
It seems to be the common ancestor of all, the father
 of things.

五章

天地不仁，以萬物為芻狗。聖人不仁，以百姓為芻狗。天地之間，其猶橐籥乎。虛而不屈，動而愈出。多言數窮，不如守中。

5

HEAVEN-and-Earth is not sentimental;
  It treats all things as straw-dogs.
The Sage is not sentimental;
He treats all his people as straw-dogs.

Between Heaven and Earth,
There seems to be a Bellows:
It is empty, and yet it is inexhaustible;
The more it works, the more comes out of it.
No amount of words can fathom it:
Better look for it within you.

六章

谷神不死是謂玄牝。玄牝之門是謂天地根。縣縣若存。用之不勤。

6

THE Spirit of the Fountain dies not.
It is called the Mysterious Feminine.
The Doorway of the Mysterious Feminine
Is called the Root of Heaven-and-Earth.

Lingering like gossamer, it has only a hint of existence;
And yet when you draw upon it, it is inexhaustible.

七章

天長地久。天地所以能長且久者。以其不自生。故能長
生。是以聖人後其身而身先。外其身而身存。非以其無
私邪。故能成其私。

7

HEAVEN lasts long, and Earth abides.
　　What is the secret of their durability?
Is it not because they do not live for themselves
That they can live so long?

Therefore, the Sage wants to remain behind,
But finds himself at the head of others;
Reckons himself out,
But finds himself safe and secure.
Is it not because he is selfless
That his Self is realized?

八章

上善若水。水善利萬物而不爭處眾人之所惡。故幾於道。居善地心善淵。與善仁言善信正善治事善能動善時。夫唯不爭故無尤。

8

THE highest form of goodness is like water.
Water knows how to benefit all things without
striving with them.
It stays in places loathed by all men.
Therefore, it comes near the Tao.

In choosing your dwelling, know how to keep to
the ground.
In cultivating your mind, know how to dive in
the hidden deeps.
In dealing with others, know how to be gentle and kind.
In speaking, know how to keep your words.
In governing, know how to maintain order.
In transacting business, know how to be efficient.
In making a move, know how to choose the right
moment.

If you do not strive with others,
You will be free from blame.

九章

持而盈之不如其已揣而梲之不可長保金玉滿堂莫之能守富貴而驕自遺其咎功遂身退天之道。

9

As for holding to fullness,
Far better were it to stop in time!

Keep on beating and sharpening a sword,
And the edge cannot be preserved for long.

Fill your house with gold and jade,
And it can no longer be guarded.

Set store by your riches and honour,
And you will only reap a crop of calamities.

Here is the Way of Heaven:
When you have done your work, retire!

十章

載營魄,抱一能無離乎。專氣致柔能嬰兒乎。滌除玄覽,能無疵乎。愛民治國能無知乎。天門開闔,能無雌乎。明白四達能無爲乎。生之畜之,生而不有。爲而不恃,長而不宰。是謂玄德。

10

IN keeping the spirit and the vital soul together,
Are you able to maintain their perfect harmony?
In gathering your vital energy to attain suppleness,
Have you reached the state of a new-born babe?
In washing and clearing your inner vision,
Have you purified it of all dross?
In loving your people and governing your state,
Are you able to dispense with cleverness?
In the opening and shutting of heaven's gate,
Are you able to play the feminine part?
Enlightened and seeing far into all directions,
Can you at the same time remain detached and
    non-active?

Rear your people!
Feed your people!
Rear them without claiming them for your own!
Do your work without setting any store by it!
Be a leader, not a butcher!
This is called hidden Virtue.

十一章

三十輻共一轂當其無，有車之用。埏埴以爲器當其無，有器之用。鑿戶牖以爲室當其無，有室之用。故有之以爲利無之以爲用。

II

THIRTY spokes converge upon a single hub;
   It is on the hole in the center that the use of
the cart hinges.

We make a vessel from a lump of clay;
It is the empty space within the vessel that makes it
   useful.

We make doors and windows for a room;
But it is these empty spaces that make the room livable.

Thus, while the tangible has advantages,
It is the intangible that makes it useful.

十二章

五色令人目盲。五音令人耳聾五味令人口爽。馳騁畋獵令人心發狂難得之貨令人行妨。是以聖人爲腹不爲目。故去彼取此

12

THE five colours blind the eye.
The five tones deafen the ear.
The five flavours cloy the palate.
Racing and hunting madden the mind.
Rare goods tempt men to do wrong.

Therefore, the Sage takes care of the belly, not the eye.
He prefers what is within to what is without.

十三章

寵辱若驚貴大患若身。何謂寵辱若驚。寵為下。得之若驚失之若驚是謂寵辱若驚。何謂貴大患若身吾所以有大患者為吾有身及吾無身吾有何患故貴以身為天下若可寄天下。愛以身為天下，若可託天下。

13

"WELCOME disgrace as a pleasant surprise.
Prize calamities as your own body."

Why should we "welcome disgrace as a pleasant
surprise"?
Because a lowly state is a boon:
Getting it is a pleasant surprise,
And so is losing it!
That is why we should "welcome disgrace as a pleasant
surprise."

Why should we "prize calamities as our own body"?
Because our body is the very source of our calamities.
If we have no body, what calamities can we have?

Hence, only he who is willing to give his body for the
sake of the world is fit to be entrusted with the world.
Only he who can do it with love is worthy of being the
steward of the world.

十四章

視之不見名曰夷。聽之不聞名曰希。搏之不得名曰微。此三者不可致詰故混而爲一。其上不皦其下不昧繩繩不可名復歸於無物是謂無狀之狀無物之象是謂惚恍迎之不見其首隨之不見其後執古之道以御今之有。能知古始是謂道紀。

14

LOOK at it but you cannot see it!
Its name is *Formless*.

Listen to it but you cannot hear it!
Its name is *Soundless*.

Grasp it but you cannot get it!
Its name is *Incorporeal*.

These three attributes are unfathomable;
Therefore they fuse into one.

Its upper side is not bright:
Its under side not dim.
Continually the Unnameable moves on,
Until it returns beyond the realm of things.
We call it the formless Form, the imageless Image.
We call it the indefinable and unimaginable.

Confront it and you do not see its face!
Follow it and you do not see its back!
Yet, equipped with this timeless Tao,
You can harness present realities.

To know the origins is initiation into the Tao.

十五章

古之善爲士者微妙玄通深不可識。夫唯不可識。故強爲之容豫焉若冬涉川。猶兮若畏四鄰。儼兮其若容渙兮若冰之將釋敦兮其若樸曠兮其若谷混兮其若濁。孰能濁以靜之徐清孰能安以久動之徐生保此道者不欲盈。夫唯不盈。故能蔽不新成。

15

THE ancient adepts of the Tao were subtle and
flexible, profound and comprehensive.
Their minds were too deep to be fathomed.

Because they are unfathomable,
One can only describe them vaguely by their
    appearance.

Hesitant like one wading a stream in winter;
Timid like one afraid of his neighbours on all sides;
Cautious and courteous like a guest;
Yielding like ice on the point of melting;
Simple like an uncarved block;
Hollow like a cave;
Confused like a muddy pool;
And yet who else could quietly and gradually evolve
    from the muddy to the clear?
Who else could slowly but steadily move from the inert
    to the living?

He who keeps the Tao does not want to be full.
But precisely because he is never full,
He can always remain like a hidden sprout,
And does not rush to early ripening.

十六章

致虛極守靜篤。萬物並作吾以觀復。夫物芸芸各復歸其根。歸根曰靜。是謂復命。復命曰常。知常曰明不知常，妄作凶知常容。容乃公。公乃王。王乃天。天乃道。道乃久。沒身不殆。

16

ATTAIN to utmost Emptiness.
Cling single-heartedly to interior peace.
While all things are stirring together,
I only contemplate the Return.
For flourishing as they do,
Each of them will return to its root.
To return to the root is to find peace.
To find peace is to fulfill one's destiny.
To fulfill one's destiny is to be constant.
To know the Constant is called Insight.

If one does not know the Constant,
One runs blindly into disasters.
If one knows the Constant,
One can understand and embrace all.
If one understands and embraces all,
One is capable of doing justice.
To be just is to be kingly;
To be kingly is to be heavenly;
To be heavenly is to be one with the Tao;
To be one with the Tao is to abide forever.
Such a one will be safe and whole
Even after the dissolution of his body.

十七章

太上下知有之。其次親而譽之。其次畏之。其次侮之。信不足焉有不信焉。悠兮其貴言功成事遂百姓皆謂我自然。

17

THE highest type of ruler is one of whose existence the people are barely aware.
Next comes one whom they love and praise.
Next comes one whom they fear.
Next comes one whom they despise and defy.

When you are lacking in faith,
Others will be unfaithful to you.

The Sage is self-effacing and scanty of words.
When his task is accomplished and things have been
  completed,
All the people say, "We ourselves have achieved it!"

十八章

大道廢，有仁義，慧智出，有大僞，六親不和，有孝慈，國家昏亂，有忠臣，

18

WHEN the Great Tao was abandoned,
   There appeared humanity and justice.
When intelligence and wit arose,
There appeared great hypocrites.
When the six relations lost their harmony,
There appeared filial piety and paternal kindness.
When darkness and disorder began to reign in a
   kingdom,
There appeared the loyal ministers.

十九章

絶聖棄智，民利百倍。絶仁棄義，民復孝慈。絶巧棄利，盜賊無有。此三者以爲文不足，故令有所屬。見素抱樸，少私寡欲。

19

DROP wisdom, abandon cleverness,
And the people will be benefited a hundredfold.

Drop humanity, abandon justice,
And the people will return to their natural affections.

Drop shrewdness, abandon sharpness,
And robbers and thieves will cease to be.

These three are the criss-cross of Tao,
And are not sufficient in themselves.
Therefore, they should be subordinated
To a Higher principle:
See the Simple and embrace the Primal,
Diminish the self and curb the desires!

二十章

絕學無憂唯之與阿相去幾何善之與惡相去若何人之所畏不可不畏荒兮其未央哉眾人熙熙如享太牢如登春臺我獨泊兮其未兆如嬰兒之未孩儽儽兮若無所歸眾人皆有餘而我獨若遺我愚人之心也哉沌沌兮俗人昭昭我獨昏昏俗人察察我獨悶悶澹兮其若海飂兮若無止眾人皆有以而我獨頑似鄙我獨異於人而貴食母

40

20

HAVE done with learning,
And you will have no more vexation.

How great is the difference between "eh" and "o"?
What is the distinction between "good" and "evil"?
Must I fear what others fear?
What abysmal nonsense this is!

All men are joyous and beaming,
As though feasting upon a sacrificial ox,
As though mounting the Spring Terrace;
I alone am placid and give no sign,
Like a babe which has not yet smiled.
I alone am forlorn as one who has no home to return to.

All men have enough and to spare:
I alone appear to possess nothing.
What a fool I am!
What a muddled mind I have!
All men are bright, bright:
I alone am dim, dim.
All men are sharp, sharp:
I alone am mum, mum!
Bland like the ocean,
Aimless like the wafting gale.

All men settle down in their grooves:
I alone am stubborn and remain outside.
But wherein I am most different from others is
In knowing to take sustenance from my Mother!

二十一章

孔德之容惟道是從。道之爲物惟恍惟惚。惚兮恍兮其中有象恍兮惚兮其中有物。窈兮冥兮其中有精其精甚真其中有信自古及今其名不去以閱衆甫吾何以知衆甫之狀哉以此。

42

21

IT lies in the nature of Grand Virtue
To follow the Tao and the Tao alone.
Now what is the Tao?
It is Something elusive and evasive.
Evasive and elusive!
And yet It contains within Itself a Form.
Elusive and evasive!
And yet It contains within Itself a Substance.
Shadowy and dim!
And yet It contains within Itself a Core of Vitality.
The Core of Vitality is very real,
It contains within Itself an unfailing Sincerity.
Throughout the ages Its Name has been preserved
In order to recall the Beginning of all things.
How do I know the ways of all things at the Beginning?
By what is within me.

二十二章

曲則全枉則直窪則盈敝則新少則得多則惑是以聖人抱一爲天下式不自見故明不自是故彰不自伐故有功不自矜故長夫唯不爭故天下莫能與之爭古之所謂曲則全者豈虛言哉誠全而歸之。

22

BEND and you will be whole.
Curl and you will be straight.
Keep empty and you will be filled.
Grow old and you will be renewed.

Have little and you will gain.
Have much and you will be confused.

Therefore, the Sage embraces the One,
And becomes a Pattern to all under Heaven.
He does not make a show of himself,
Hence he shines;
Does not justify himself,
Hence he becomes known;
Does not boast of his ability,
Hence he gets his credit;
Does not brandish his success,
Hence he endures;
Does not compete with anyone,
Hence no one can compete with him.
Indeed, the ancient saying: "Bend and you will remain
    whole" is no idle word.
Nay, if you have really attained wholeness, everything
    will flock to you.

二十三章

希言自然。故飄風不終朝。驟雨不終日。孰爲此者天地。天地尚不能久而況於人乎。故從事於道者道者同於道。德者同於德。失者同於失。同於道者道亦樂得之。同於德者德亦樂得之。同於失者失亦樂得之。信不足焉，有不信焉。

46

23

ONLY simple and quiet words will ripen of
themselves.
For a whirlwind does not last a whole morning,
Nor does a sudden shower last a whole day.
Who is their author? Heaven-and-Earth!
Even Heaven-and-Earth cannot make such violent things
last long;
How much truer is it of the rash endeavours of men?

Hence, he who cultivates the Tao is one with the Tao;
He who practices Virtue is one with Virtue;
And he who courts after Loss is one with Loss.

To be one with the Tao is to be a welcome accession
to the Tao;
To be one with Virtue is to be a welcome accession
to Virtue;
To be one with Loss is to be a welcome accession
to Loss.

Deficiency of faith on your part
Entails faithlessness on the part of others.

二十四章

企者不立跨者不行自見者不明自是者不彰自伐者
無功自矜者不長其在道也曰餘食贅行物或惡之故
有道者不處。

24

ONE on tip-toe cannot stand.
One astride cannot walk.
One who displays himself does not shine.
One who justifies himself has no glory.
One who boasts of his own ability has no merit.
One who parades his own success will not endure.
In Tao these things are called "unwanted food and
  extraneous growths,"
Which are loathed by all things.
Hence, a man of Tao does not set his heart upon them.

二十五章

有物混成。先天地生。寂兮寥兮。獨立不改。周行而不殆。可以爲天下母。吾不知其名。字之曰道。強爲之名曰大。大曰逝。逝曰遠。遠曰反。故道大、天大、地大、王亦大。域中有四大。而王居其一焉。人法地。地法天。天法道。道法自然。

50

25

THERE was Something undefined and yet complete in
itself,
Born before Heaven-and-Earth.

Silent and boundless,
Standing alone without change,
Yet pervading all without fail,
It may be regarded as the Mother of the world.
I do not know its name;
I style it "Tao";
And, in the absence of a better word, call it
   "The Great."

To be great is to go on,
To go on is to be far,
To be far is to return.

Hence, "Tao is great,
Heaven is great,
Earth is great,
King is great."
Thus, the king is one of the great four in the Universe.

Man follows the ways of the Earth.
The Earth follows the ways of Heaven,
Heaven follows the ways of Tao,
Tao follows its own ways.

二十六章

重爲輕根。靜爲躁君。是以聖人終日行不離輜重。雖有榮觀,燕處超然。奈何萬乘之主而以身輕天下。輕則失本。躁則失君。

26

HEAVINESS is the root of lightness.
Serenity is the master of restlessness.

Therefore, the Sage, travelling all day,
Does not part with the baggage-wagon;
Though there may be gorgeous sights to see,
He stays at ease in his own home.

Why should a lord of ten thousand chariots
Display his lightness to the world?
To be light is to be separated from one's root;
To be restless is to lose one's self-mastery.

二十七章

善行無轍迹善言無瑕讁善數不用籌策善閉無關楗而不可開善結無繩約而不可解是以聖人常善救人故無棄人常善救物故無棄物是謂襲明故善人者不善人之師不善人者善人之資不貴其師不愛其資雖智大迷是謂要妙。

54

27

GOOD walking leaves no track behind it;
Good speech leaves no mark to be picked at;
Good calculation makes no use of counting-slips;
Good shutting makes no use of bolt and bar,
And yet nobody can undo it;
Good tying makes no use of rope and knot,
And yet nobody can untie it.

Hence, the Sage is always good at saving men,
And therefore nobody is abandoned;
Always good at saving things,
And therefore nothing is wasted.

This is called "following the guidance of the Inner
   Light."

Hence, good men are teachers of bad men,
While bad men are the charge of good men.
Not to revere one's teacher,
Not to cherish one's charge,
Is to be on the wrong road, however intelligent one
   may be.
This is an essential tenet of the Tao.

二十八章

知其雄守其雌，爲天下谿。爲天下谿，常德不離，復歸於嬰兒。知其白守其黑，爲天下式。爲天下式，常德不忒，復歸於無極。知其榮守其辱，爲天下谷。爲天下谷，常德乃足，復歸於樸。樸散則爲器。聖人用之，則爲官長。故大制不割。

56

28

KNOW the masculine,
Keep to the feminine,
And be the Brook of the World.
To be the Brook of the World is
To move constantly in the path of Virtue
Without swerving from it,
And to return again to infancy.

Know the white,
Keep to the black,
And be the Pattern of the World.
To be the Pattern of the World is
To move constantly in the path of Virtue
Without erring a single step,
And to return again to the Infinite.

Know the glorious,
Keep to the lowly,
And be the Fountain of the World.
To be the Fountain of the World is
To live the abundant life of Virtue,
And to return again to Primal Simplicity.

When Primal Simplicity diversifies,
It becomes useful vessels,
Which, in the hands of the Sage, become officers.
Hence, "a great tailor does little cutting."

二十九章

將欲取天下而爲之。吾見其不得已。天下神器不可爲也。爲者敗之執者失之故物或行或隨或歔或吹或强或羸或挫或隳是以聖人去甚去奢去泰。

29

DOES anyone want to take the world and do what he
wants with it?
I do not see how he can succeed.

The world is a sacred vessel, which must not be
tampered with or grabbed after.
To tamper with it is to spoil it, and to grasp it is to
lose it.

In fact, for all things there is a time for going ahead, and
a time for following behind;
A time for slow-breathing and a time for fast-breathing;
A time to grow in strength and a time to decay;
A time to be up and a time to be down.

Therefore, the Sage avoids all extremes, excesses and
extravagances.

三十章

以道佐人主者不以兵強天下。其事好還。師之所處、荆棘生焉。大軍之後必有凶年。善者果而已。不敢以取强。果而勿矜。果而勿伐。果而勿驕。果而不得已。果而勿强。物壯則老。是謂不道。不道早已。

30

He who knows how to guide a ruler in the path of Tao
Does not try to override the world with force of arms.
It is in the nature of a military weapon to turn against its
    wielder.

Wherever armies are stationed, thorny bushes grow.
After a great war, bad years invariably follow.

What you want is to protect efficiently your own state,
But not to aim at self-aggrandisement.

After you have attained your purpose,
You must not parade your success,
You must not boast of your ability,
You must not feel proud,
You must rather regret that you had not been able to
    prevent the war.
You must never think of conquering others by force.

For to be over-developed is to hasten decay,
And this is against Tao,
And what is against Tao will soon cease to be.

三十一章

夫佳兵者不祥之器物或惡之故有道者不處君子居則貴左用兵則貴右兵者不祥之器非君子之器不得已而用之恬淡爲上勝而不美而美之者是樂殺人夫樂殺人者則不可以得志於天下矣吉事尚左凶事尚右偏將軍居左上將軍居右言以喪禮處之殺人之衆以哀悲泣之戰勝以喪禮處之

31

FINE weapons of war augur evil.
Even things seem to hate them.
Therefore, a man of Tao does not set his heart
upon them.

In ordinary life, a gentleman regards the left side
as the place of honour:
In war, the right side is the place of honour.

As weapons are instruments of evil,
They are not properly a gentleman's instruments;
Only on necessity will he resort to them.
For peace and quiet are dearest to his heart,
And to him even a victory is no cause for rejoicing.

To rejoice over a victory is to rejoice over the slaughter
of men!
Hence a man who rejoices over the slaughter of men
cannot expect to thrive in the world of men.

On happy occasions the left side is preferred:
On sad occasions the right side.
In the army, the Lieutenant Commander stands on
the left,
While the Commander-in-Chief stands on the right.
This means that war is treated on a par with a funeral
service.
Because many people have been killed, it is only right
that survivors should mourn for them.
Hence, even a victory is a funeral.

三十二章

道常無名。樸雖小天下莫能臣也。侯王若能守之、萬物將自賓。天地相合以降甘露民莫之令而自均。始制有名名亦既有夫亦將知止。知止可以不殆譬道之在天下。猶川谷之於江海。

32

Tao is always nameless.
  Small as it is in its Primal Simplicity,
It is inferior to nothing in the world.
If only a ruler could cling to it,
Everything will render homage to him.
Heaven and Earth will be harmonized
And send down sweet dew.
Peace and order will reign among the people
Without any command from above.

When once the Primal Simplicity diversified,
Different names appeared.
Are there not enough names now?

Is this not the time to stop?
To know when to stop is to preserve ourselves from
  danger.
The Tao is to the world what a great river or an ocean
  is to the streams and brooks.

三十三章

知人者智。自知者明。勝人者有力。自勝者強。知足者富。強行者有志。不失其所者久。死而不亡者壽。

33

HE who knows men is clever;
He who knows himself has insight.
He who conquers men has force;
He who conquers himself is truly strong.

He who knows when he has got enough is rich,
And he who adheres assiduously to the path of Tao is
 a man of steady purpose.
He who stays where he has found his true home endures
 long,
And he who dies but perishes not enjoys real longevity.

三十四章

大道氾兮其可左右。萬物恃之而生而不辭。功成不名
有。衣養萬物而不爲主。常無欲，可名於小，萬物歸焉而
不爲主，可名爲大。以其終不自爲大，故能成其大。

34

THE Great Tao is universal like a flood.
How can it be turned to the right or to the left?

All creatures depend on it,
And it denies nothing to anyone.

It does its work,
But it makes no claims for itself.

It clothes and feeds all,
But it does not lord it over them:
Thus, it may be called "the Little."

All things return to it as to their home,
But it does not lord it over them:
Thus, it may be called "the Great."

It is just because it does not wish to be great
That its greatness is fully realized.

三十五章

執大象，天下往往而不害，安平太。樂與餌，過客止。道之出口，淡乎其無味，視之不足見。聽之不足聞。用之不足既。

35

HE who holds the Great Symbol will attract all things to him.
They flock to him and receive no harm, for in him they find peace, security and happiness.

Music and dainty dishes can only make a passing guest pause.
But the words of Tao possess lasting effects,
Though they are mild and flavourless,
Though they appeal neither to the eye nor to the ear.

三十六章

將欲歙之、必固張之。將欲弱之、必固強之。將欲廢之、必固興之。將欲奪之、必固與之。是謂微明。柔弱勝剛強魚不可脫於淵國之利器不可以示人

36

WHAT is in the end to be shrunken,
  Begins by being first stretched out.
What is in the end to be weakened,
Begins by being first made strong.
What is in the end to be thrown down,
Begins by being first set on high.
What is in the end to be despoiled,
Begins by being first richly endowed.

Herein is the subtle wisdom of life:
The soft and weak overcomes the hard and strong.

Just as the fish must not leave the deeps,
So the ruler must not display his weapons.

三十七章

道常無爲而無不爲。侯王若能守之，萬物將自化。化而欲作，吾將鎮之以無名之樸。無名之樸，夫亦將無欲。不欲以靜，天下將自定。

37

TAO never makes any ado,
  And yet it does everything.
If a ruler can cling to it,
All things will grow of themselves.
When they have grown and tend to make a stir,
It is time to keep them in their place by the aid of the
    nameless Primal Simplicity,
Which alone can curb the desires of men.
When the desires of men are curbed, there will be peace,
And the world will settle down of its own accord.

三十八章

上德不德，是以有德。下德不失德，是以無德。上德無爲，而無以爲。下德爲之，而有以爲。上仁爲之，而無以爲。上義爲之，而有以爲。上禮爲之，而莫之應，則攘臂而扔之。故失道而後德。失德而後仁。失仁而後義。失義而後禮。夫禮者，忠信之薄，而亂之首。前識者，道之華，而愚之始。是以大丈夫處其厚，不居其薄。處其實，不居其華。故去彼取此。

38

HIGH Virtue is non-virtuous;
Therefore it has Virtue.
Low Virtue never frees itself from virtuousness;
Therefore it has no Virtue.

High Virtue makes no fuss and has no private ends
    to serve:
Low Virtue not only fusses but has private ends to serve.

High humanity fusses but has no private ends to serve:
High morality not only fusses but has private ends
    to serve.
High ceremony fusses but finds no response;
Then it tries to enforce itself with rolled-up sleeves.

Failing Tao, man resorts to Virtue.
Failing Virtue, man resorts to humanity.
Failing humanity, man resorts to morality.
Failing morality, man resorts to ceremony.
Now, ceremony is the merest husk of faith and loyalty;
It is the beginning of all confusion and disorder.

As to foreknowledge, it is only the flower of Tao,
And the beginning of folly.

Therefore, the full-grown man sets his heart upon
    the substance rather than the husk;
Upon the fruit rather than the flower.
Truly, he prefers what is within to what is without.

三十九章

昔之得一者天得一以清。地得一以寧神得一以靈谷得一以盈萬物得一以生侯王得一以爲天下貞其致之天無以清將恐裂地無以寧將恐發神無以靈將恐歇谷無以盈將恐竭萬物無以生將恐滅侯王無以貴高將恐蹶。故貴以賤爲本高以下爲基是以侯王自謂孤寡不穀此非以賤爲本邪非乎。

39

FROM of old there are not lacking things that have
 attained Oneness.
The sky attained Oneness and became clear;
The earth attained Oneness and became calm;
The spirits attained Oneness and became charged with
 mystical powers;
The fountains attained Oneness and became full;
The ten thousand creatures attained Oneness and
 became reproductive;
Barons and princes attained Oneness and became
 sovereign rulers of the world.
All of them are what they are by virtue of Oneness.

If the sky were not clear, it would be likely to fall to
 pieces;
If the earth were not calm, it would be likely to burst
 into bits;
If the spirits were not charged with mystical powers,
 they would be likely to cease from being;
If the fountains were not full, they would be likely to
 dry up;
If the ten thousand creatures were not reproductive, they
 would be likely to come to extinction;
If the barons and princes were not the sovereign rulers,
 they would be likely to stumble and fall.

Truly, humility is the root from which greatness springs,
And the high must be built upon the foundation of the
 low.
That is why barons and princes style themselves
 "The Helpless One," "The Little One," and
 "The Worthless One."

故致數輿無輿。不欲琭琭如玉。珞珞如石。

Perhaps they too realize their dependence upon
  the lowly.

Truly, too much honour means no honour.
It is not wise to shine like jade and resound like
  stone-chimes.

四十章

反者道之動。弱者道之用天下萬物生於有。有生於無。

40

THE movement of the Tao consists in Returning.
The use of the Tao consists in softness.

All things under heaven are born of the corporeal:
The corporeal is born of the Incorporeal.

四十一章

上士聞道勤而行之中士聞道若存若亡下士聞道大笑之不笑不足以爲道故建言有之明道若昧進道若退夷道若纇上德若谷大白若辱廣德若不足建德若偷質真若渝大方無隅大器晚成大音希聲大象無形道隱無名夫唯道善貸且成

41

WHEN a wise scholar hears the Tao,
He practises it diligently.
When a mediocre scholar hears the Tao,
He wavers between belief and unbelief.
When a worthless scholar hears the Tao,
He laughs boisterously at it.
But if such a one does not laugh at it,
The Tao would not be the Tao!

The wise men of old have truly said:

> The bright Way looks dim.
> The progressive Way looks retrograde.
> The smooth Way looks rugged.
> High Virtue looks like an abyss.
> Great whiteness looks spotted.
> Abundant Virtue looks deficient.
> Established Virtue looks shabby.
> Solid Virtue looks as though melted.
> Great squareness has no corners.
> Great talents ripen late.
> Great sound is silent.
> Great Form is shapeless.

The Tao is hidden and nameless;
Yet it alone knows how to render help and to fulfill.

四十二章

道生一。一生二。二生三。三生萬物。萬物負陰而抱陽冲

氣以爲和。人之所惡唯孤寡不穀而王公以爲稱故物

或損之而益或益之而損人之所教我亦教之強梁者

不得其死吾將以爲教父。

42

TAO gave birth to One,
  One gave birth to Two,
Two gave birth to Three,
Three gave birth to all the myriad things.

All the myriad things carry the *Yin* on their backs and
  hold the *Yang* in their embrace,
Deriving their vital harmony from the proper blending
  of the two vital Breaths.

What is more loathed by men than to be "helpless,"
  "little," and "worthless"?
And yet these are the very names the princes and barons
  call themselves.

Truly, one may gain by losing;
And one may lose by gaining.

What another has taught let me repeat:
"A man of violence will come to a violent end."
Whoever said this can be my teacher and my father.

四十三章

天下之至柔馳騁天下之至堅。無有入無間。吾是以知無爲之有益不言之教。無爲之益天下希及之。

43

THE softest of all things
  Overrides the hardest of all things.
Only Nothing can enter into no-space.
Hence I know the advantages of Non-Ado.

Few things under heaven are as instructive as
  the lessons of Silence,
Or as beneficial as the fruits of Non-Ado.

四十四章

名與身孰親。身與貨孰多。得與亡孰病。是故甚愛必大費。多藏必厚亡。知足不辱知止不殆可以長久。

44

As for your name and your body, which is the dearer?
As for your body and your wealth, which is the more to be prized?
As for gain and loss, which is the more painful?

Thus, an excessive love for anything will cost you dear in the end.
The storing up of too much goods will entail a heavy loss.

To know when you have enough is to be immune from disgrace.
To know when to stop is to be preserved from perils.
Only thus can you endure long.

四十五章

大成若缺。其用不弊。大盈若冲其用不窮。大直若屈。大巧若拙。大辯若訥。躁勝寒。靜勝熱。清靜爲天下正。

45

THE greatest perfection seems imperfect,
And yet its use is inexhaustible.
The greatest fullness seems empty,
And yet its use is endless.

The greatest straightness looks like crookedness.
The greatest skill appears clumsy.
The greatest eloquence sounds like stammering.

Restlessness overcomes cold,
But calm overcomes heat.

The peaceful and serene
Is the Norm of the World.

四十六章

天下有道，卻走馬以糞。天下無道，戎馬生於郊。禍莫大於不知足。咎莫大於欲得。故知足之足常足矣。

46

WHEN the world is in possession of the Tao,
  The galloping horses are led to fertilize the fields
with their droppings.
When the world has become Taoless,
War horses breed themselves on the suburbs.

There is no calamity like not knowing what is enough.
There is no evil like covetousness.
Only he who knows what is enough will always have
  enough.

四十七章

不出戶，知天下。不闚牖見天道。其出彌遠，其知彌少。是以聖人不行而知。不見而名不爲而成。

47

WITHOUT going out of your door,
  You can know the ways of the world.
Without peeping through your window,
You can see the Way of Heaven.
The farther you go,
The less you know.

Thus, the Sage knows without travelling,
Sees without looking,
And achieves without Ado.

四十八章

爲學日益爲道日損損之又損以至於無爲無爲而無不爲。取天下常以無事及其有事不足以取天下。

48

LEARNING consists in daily accumulating;
The practice of Tao consists in daily diminishing.

Keep on diminishing and diminishing,
Until you reach the state of Non-Ado.
No-Ado, and yet nothing is left undone.

To win the world, one must renounce all.
If one still has private ends to serve,
One will never be able to win the world.

四十九章

聖人無常心。以百姓心爲心。善者吾善之不善者吾亦善之。德善信者吾信之不信者吾亦信之。德信聖人在天下歙歙爲天下渾其心聖人皆孩之。

49

THE Sage has no interests of his own,
But takes the interests of the people as his own.
He is kind to the kind;
He is also kind to the unkind:
For Virtue is kind.
He is faithful to the faithful;
He is also faithful to the unfaithful:
For Virtue is faithful.

In the midst of the world, the Sage is shy and
self-effacing.
For the sake of the world he keeps his heart in its
nebulous state.
All the people strain their ears and eyes:
The Sage only smiles like an amused infant.

五十章

出生入死生之徒十有三死之徒十有三人之生動之
死地亦十有三夫何故以其生生之厚蓋聞善攝生者
陸行不遇虎兕入軍不被甲兵兕無所投其角虎無所
措其爪兵無所容其刃夫何故以其無死地

50

WHEN one is out of Life, one is in Death. The companions of life are thirteen; the companions of Death are thirteen; and, when a living person moves into the Realm of Death, his companions are also thirteen. How is this? Because he draws upon the resources of Life too heavily.

It is said that he who knows well how to live meets no tigers or wild buffaloes on his road, and comes out from the battle-ground untouched by the weapons of war. For, in him, a buffalo would find no butt for his horns, a tiger nothing to lay his claws upon, and a weapon of war no place to admit its point. How is this? Because there is no room for Death in him.

五十一章

道生之德畜之物形之勢成之是以萬物莫不尊道而貴德道之尊德之貴夫莫之命而常自然故道生之德畜之長之育之亭之毒之養之覆之生而不有為而不恃長而不宰是謂玄德

51

Tao gives them life,
Virtue nurses them,
Matter shapes them,
Environment perfects them.
Therefore all things without exception worship Tao and
do homage to Virtue.
They have not been commanded to worship Tao and do
homage to Virtue,
But they always do so spontaneously.

It is Tao that gives them life:
It is Virtue that nurses them, grows them, fosters them,
shelters them, comforts them, nourishes them, and
covers them under her wings.
To give life but to claim nothing,
To do your work but to set no store by it,
To be a leader, not a butcher,
This is called hidden Virtue.

五十二章

天下有始，以爲天下母。既得其母，以知其子。既知其子，復守其母。沒身不殆。塞其兌，閉其門，終身不勤。開其兌，濟其事，終身不救。見小曰明，守柔曰强。用其光，復歸其明。無遺身殃，是謂習常。

52

ALL-under-Heaven have a common Beginning.
This Beginning is the Mother of the world.
Having known the Mother,
We may proceed to know her children.
Having known the children,
We should go back and hold on to the Mother.
In so doing, you will incur no risk
Even though your body be annihilated.

Block all the passages!
Shut all the doors!
And to the end of your days you will not be worn out.
Open the passages!
Multiply your activities!
And to the end of your days you will remain helpless.

To see the small is to have insight.
To hold on to weakness is to be strong.
Use the lights, but return to your insight.
Do not bring calamities upon yourself.
This is the way of cultivating the Changeless.

五十三章

使我介然有知行於大道唯施是畏大道甚夷而民好徑朝甚除田甚蕪倉甚虛服文綵帶利劍厭飲食財貨有餘是謂盜夸非道也哉。

53

IF only I had the tiniest grain of wisdom,
I should walk in the Great Way,
And my only fear would be to stray from it.

The Great Way is very smooth and straight;
And yet the people prefer devious paths.

The court is very clean and well garnished,
But the fields are very weedy and wild,
And the granaries are very empty!
They wear gorgeous clothes,
They carry sharp swords,
They surfeit themselves with food and drink,
They possess more riches than they can use!
They are the heralds of brigandage!
As for Tao, what do they know about it?

善建者不拔。善抱者不脫。子孫以祭祀不輟。修之於身。
其德乃眞。修之於家。其德乃餘。修之於鄉。其德乃長。修
之於國。其德乃豐。修之於天下。其德乃普。故以身觀身。
以家觀家。以鄉觀鄉。以國觀國。以天下觀天下。吾何以
知天下然哉以此。

五十四章

54

WHAT is well planted cannot be uprooted.
What is well embraced cannot slip away.
Your descendants will carry on the ancestral sacrifice for
generations without end.

Cultivate Virtue in your own person,
And it becomes a genuine part of you.
Cultivate it in the family,
And it will abide.
Cultivate it in the community,
And it will live and grow.
Cultivate it in the state,
And it will flourish abundantly.
Cultivate it in the world,
And it will become universal.

Hence, a person must be judged as person;
A family as family;
A community as community;
A state as state;
The world as world.

How do I know about the world?
By what is within me.

五十五章

含德之厚、比於赤子。蜂蠆虺蛇不螫、猛獸不據、攫鳥不搏。骨弱筋柔而握固。未知牝牡之合而全作、精之至也。終日號而不嗄、和之至也。知和曰常、知常曰明。益生曰祥。心使氣曰強。物壯則老、謂之不道、不道早已。

55

ONE who is steeped in Virtue is akin to the
new-born babe.
Wasps and poisonous serpents do not sting it,
Nor fierce beasts seize it,
Nor birds of prey maul it.
Its bones are tender, its sinews soft,
But its grip is firm.
It has not known the union of the male and the female,
Growing in its wholeness, and keeping its vitality in its
    perfect integrity.
It howls and screams all day long without getting hoarse,
Because it embodies perfect harmony.

To know harmony is to know the Changeless.
To know the Changeless is to have insight.

To hasten the growth of life is ominous.
To control the breath by the will is to overstrain it.
To be overgrown is to decay.
All this is against Tao,
And whatever is against Tao soon ceases to be.

五十六章

知者不言言者不知。塞其兌閉其門挫其銳解其分和其光同其塵是謂玄同。故不可得而親不可得而疏不可得而利不可得而害不可得而貴不可得而賤故為天下貴。

56

HE who knows does not speak.
He who speaks does not know.

Block all the passages!
Shut all the doors!
Blunt all edges!
Untie all tangles!
Harmonize all lights!
Unite the world into one whole!
This is called the Mystical Whole,
Which you cannot court after nor shun,
Benefit nor harm, honour nor humble.

Therefore, it is the Highest of the world.

五十七章

以正治國以奇用兵以無事取天下吾何以知其然哉。以此。天下多忌諱而民彌貧民多利器國家滋昏人多伎巧奇物滋起法令滋彰盜賊多有故聖人云我無爲而民自化我好靜而民自正我無事而民自富我無欲而民自樸。

57

You govern a kingdom by normal rules;
You fight a war by exceptional moves;
But you win the world by letting alone.
How do I know that this is so?
By what is within me!

The more taboos and inhibitions there are in the world,
The poorer the people become.
The sharper the weapons the people possess,
The greater confusion reigns in the realm.
The more clever and crafty the men,
The oftener strange things happen.
The more articulate the laws and ordinances,
The more robbers and thieves arise.

Therefore, the Sage says:
I do not make any fuss, and the people transform
    themselves.
I love quietude, and the people settle down in their
    regular grooves.
I do not engage myself in anything, and the people
    grow rich.
I have no desires, and the people return to
    Simplicity.

五十八章

其政悶悶，其民淳淳，其政察察，其民缺缺。禍兮福之所倚，福兮禍之所伏。孰知其極，其無正正復爲奇，善復爲妖。人之迷其日固久。是以聖人方而不割，廉而不劌，直而不肆，光而不燿。

118

58

WHERE the ruler is mum, mum,
   The people are simple and happy.
Where the ruler is sharp, sharp,
The people are wily and discontented.

Bad fortune is what good fortune leans on,
Good fortune is what bad fortune hides in.
Who knows the ultimate end of this process?
Is there no norm of right?
Yet what is normal soon becomes abnormal,
And what is auspicious soon turns ominous.
Long indeed have the people been in a quandary.

Therefore, the Sage squares without cutting,
   carves without disfiguring,
   straightens without straining,
   enlightens without dazzling.

五十九章

治人事天，莫若嗇。夫唯嗇，是謂早服。早服謂之重積德。重積德則無不克，無不克則莫知其極，莫知其極可以有國。有國之母，可以長久。是謂深根固柢，長生久視之道。

59

IN governing a people and in serving Heaven,
There is nothing like frugality.
To be frugal is to return before straying.
To return before straying is to have a double reserve
    of Virtue.
To have a double reserve of Virtue is to overcome
    everything.
To overcome everything is to reach an invisible height.
Only he who has reached an invisible height can have
    a kingdom.
Only he who has got the Mother of a kingdom can
    last long.
This is the way to be deep-rooted and firm-planted
    in the Tao,
The secret of long life and lasting vision.

六十章

治大國若烹小鮮。以道蒞天下，其鬼不神。非其鬼不神。其神不傷人。非其神不傷人。聖人亦不傷人。夫兩不相傷。故德交歸焉。

60

RULING a big kingdom is like cooking a small fish. When a man of Tao reigns over the world, demons have no spiritual powers. Not that the demons have no spiritual powers, but the spirits themselves do no harm to men. Not that the spirits do no harm to men, but the Sage himself does no harm to his people. If only the ruler and his people would refrain from harming each other, all the benefits of life would accumulate in the kingdom.

六十一章

大國者下流天下之交天下之牝牝常以靜勝牡以靜
爲下，故大國以下小國則取小國小國以下大國則取
大國故或下以取或下而取大國不過欲兼畜人小國
不過欲入事人夫兩者各得其所欲大者宜爲下。

61

A GREAT country is like the lowland toward which all streams flow. It is the Reservoir of all under heaven, the Feminine of the world.

The Feminine always conquers the Masculine by her quietness, by lowering herself through her quietness.

Hence, if a great country can lower itself before a small country, it will win over the small country; and if a small country can lower itself before a great country, it will win over the great country. The one wins by stooping; the other, by remaining low.

What a great country wants is simply to embrace more people; and what a small country wants is simply to come to serve its patron. Thus, each gets what it wants. But it behooves a great country to lower itself.

六十二章

道者萬物之奧善人之寶不善人之所保美言可以市。尊行可以加人人之不善何棄之有故立天子置三公雖有拱璧以先駟馬不如坐進此道古之所以貴此道者何不曰以求得有罪以免邪故爲天下貴。

62

THE Tao is the hidden Reservoir of all things.
A treasure to the honest, it is a safeguard to
the erring.

A good word will find its own market.
A good deed may be used as a gift to another.
That a man is straying from the right path
Is no reason that he should be cast away.

Hence, at the Enthronement of an Emperor,
Or at the Installation of the Three Ministers,
Let others offer their discs of jade, following it up
with teams of horses;
It is better for you to offer the Tao without moving
your feet!

Why did the ancients prize the Tao?
Is it not because by virtue of it he who seeks finds,
And the guilty are forgiven?
That is why it is such a treasure to the world.

六十三章

爲無爲事無事味無味大小多少報怨以德。圖難於其易爲大於其細。天下難事必作於易天下大事必作於細。是以聖人終不爲大，故能成其大。夫輕諾必寡信多易必多難。是以聖人猶難之。故終無難矣。

63

Do the Non-Ado.
Strive for the effortless.
Savour the savourless.
Exalt the low.
Multiply the few.
Requite injury with kindness.

Nip troubles in the bud.
Sow the great in the small.

Difficult things of the world
Can only be tackled when they are easy.
Big things of the world
Can only be achieved by attending to their small
  beginnings.
Thus, the Sage never has to grapple with big things,
Yet he alone is capable of achieving them!

He who promises lightly must be lacking in faith.
He who thinks everything easy will end by finding
  everything difficult.
Therefore, the Sage, who regards everything as difficult,
Meets with no difficulties in the end.

六十四章

其安易持其未兆易謀其脆易泮其微易散爲之於未有治之於未亂合抱之木生於毫末九層之臺起於累土千里之行始於足下爲者敗之執者失之是以聖人無爲故無敗無執故無失民之從事常於幾成而敗之慎終如始則無敗事是以聖人欲不欲不貴難得之貨學不學復衆人之所過以輔萬物之自然而不敢爲。

130

64

WHAT is at rest is easy to hold.
What manifests no omens is easily forestalled.
What is fragile is easily shattered.
What is small is easily scattered.

Tackle things before they have appeared.
Cultivate peace and order before confusion and disorder
 have set in.

A tree as big as a man's embrace springs from a tiny
 sprout.
A tower nine stories high begins with a heap of earth.
A journey of a thousand leagues starts from where your
 feet stand.

He who fusses over anything spoils it.
He who grasps anything loses it.
The Sage fusses over nothing and therefore spoils
 nothing.
He grips at nothing and therefore loses nothing.

In handling affairs, people often spoil them just
 at the point of success.
With heedfulness in the beginning and patience
 at the end, nothing will be spoiled.

Therefore, the Sage desires to be desireless,
Sets no value on rare goods,
Learns to unlearn his learning,
And induces the masses to return from where
 they have overpassed.
He only helps all creatures to find their own nature,
But does not venture to lead them by the nose.

六十五章

古之善爲道者，非以明民，將以愚之。民之難治，以其智多。故以智治國，國之賊。不以智治國，國之福。知此兩者亦稽式。常知稽式，是謂玄德。玄德深矣遠矣，與物反矣，然後乃至大順。

65

IN the old days, those who were well versed in the practice of the Tao did not try to enlighten the people, but rather to keep them in the state of simplicity. For, why are the people hard to govern? Because they are too clever! Therefore, he who governs his state with cleverness is its malefactor; but he who governs his state without resorting to cleverness is its benefactor. To know these principles is to possess a rule and a measure. To keep the rule and the measure constantly in your mind is what we call Mystical Virtue. Deep and far-reaching is Mystical Virtue! It leads all things to return, till they come back to Great Harmony!

六十六章

江海所以能爲百谷王者，以其善下之，故能爲百谷王。

是以欲上民必以言下之，欲先民必以身後之，是以聖人處上而民不重，處前而民不害，是以天下樂推而不厭。

以其不爭，故天下莫能與之爭。

66

How does the sea become the king of all streams?
  Because it lies lower than they!
Hence it is the king of all streams.

Therefore, the Sage reigns over the people by humbling
  himself in speech;
And leads the people by putting himself behind.

Thus it is that when a Sage stands above the people,
  they do not feel the heaviness of his weight;
And when he stands in front of the people, they do not
  feel hurt.
Therefore all the world is glad to push him forward
  without getting tired of him.

Just because he strives with nobody,
Nobody can ever strive with him.

六十七章

天下皆謂我道大似不肖。夫唯大故似不肖。若肖久矣其細也夫。我有三寶持而保之。一曰慈二曰儉三曰不敢爲天下先。慈故能勇儉故能廣不敢爲天下先故能成器長。今舍慈且勇舍儉且廣舍後且先死矣。夫慈以戰則勝以守則固天將救之以慈衛之。

67

ALL the world says that my Tao is great, but seems queer, like nothing on earth. But it is just because my Tao is great that it is like nothing on earth! If it were like anything on earth, how small it would have been from the very beginning!

I have Three Treasures, which I hold fast and watch over closely. The first is *Mercy*. The second is *Frugality*. The third is *Not Daring to Be First in the World*. Because I am merciful, therefore I can be brave. Because I am frugal, therefore I can be generous. Because I dare not be first, therefore I can be the chief of all vessels.

If a man wants to be brave without first being merciful, generous without first being frugal, a leader without first wishing to follow, he is only courting death!

Mercy alone can help you to win a war. Mercy alone can help you to defend your state. For Heaven will come to the rescue of the merciful, and protect him with *its* Mercy.

六十八章

善爲士者不武。善戰者不怒。善勝敵者不與。善用人者爲之下。是謂不爭之德。是謂用人之力。是謂配天古之極。

68

A GOOD soldier is never aggressive;
A good fighter is never angry.
The best way of conquering an enemy
Is to win him over by not antagonizing him.
The best way of employing a man
Is to serve under him.
This is called the virtue of non-striving!
This is called using the abilities of men!
This is called being wedded to Heaven as of old!

六十九章

用兵有言吾不敢爲主而爲客不敢進寸而退尺是謂行無行。攘無臂扔無敵執無兵禍莫大於輕敵輕敵幾喪吾寶故抗兵相加哀者勝矣

69

THE strategists have a saying:
 I dare not be a host, but rather a guest;
  I dare not advance an inch, but rather retreat a foot.

This is called marching without moving,
Rolling up one's sleeves without baring one's arms,
Capturing the enemy without confronting him,
Holding a weapon that is invisible.

There is no greater calamity than to under-estimate
 the strength of your enemy.
For to under-estimate the strength of your enemy is
to lose your treasure.

Therefore, when opposing troops meet in battle,
 victory belongs to the grieving side.

七十章

吾言甚易知甚易行天下莫能知莫能行言有宗事有君。夫唯無知是以不我知知我者希則我者貴是以聖人被褐懷玉。

70

MY words are very easy to understand, and very
easy to practise:
But the world cannot understand them, nor practise
  them.

My words have an Ancestor.
My deeds have a Lord.
The people have no knowledge of this.
Therefore, they have no knowledge of me.

The fewer persons know me,
The nobler are they that follow me.
Therefore, the Sage wears coarse clothes,
While keeping the jade in his bosom.

七十一章

知不知上。不知知病。夫唯病病，是以不病。聖人不病，以其病病，是以不病。

71

To realize that our knowledge is ignorance,
This is a noble insight.
To regard our ignorance as knowledge,
This is mental sickness.

Only when we are sick of our sickness
Shall we cease to be sick.
The Sage is not sick, being sick of sickness;
This is the secret of health.

七十二章

民不畏威則大威至。無狎其所居無厭其所生夫唯不厭。是以不厭是以聖人自知不自見自愛不自貴故去彼取此。

72

WHEN the people no longer fear your power,
It is a sign that a greater power is coming.

Interfere not lightly with their dwelling,
Nor lay heavy burdens upon their livelihood.
Only when you cease to weary them,
They will cease to be wearied of you.

Therefore, the Sage knows himself,
But makes no show of himself;
Loves himself,
But does not exalt himself.
He prefers what is within to what is without.

七十三章

勇於敢則殺。勇於不敢則活。此兩者或利或害。天之所
惡，孰知其故。是以聖人猶難之。天之道，不爭而善勝，不
言而善應。不召而自來。繟然而善謀。天網恢恢，疏而不
失。

73

He who is brave in daring will be killed;
He who is brave in not daring will survive.
Of these two kinds of bravery, one is beneficial,
  while the other proves harmful.
Some things are detested by Heaven,
But who knows the reason?
Even the Sage is baffled by such a question.

It is Heaven's Way to conquer without striving,
To get responses without speaking,
To induce the people to come without summoning,
To act according to plans without haste.

Vast is Heaven's net;
Sparse-meshed it is, and yet
Nothing can slip through it.

七十四章

民不畏死。奈何以死懼之。若使民常畏死而爲奇者,吾得執而殺之,孰敢。常有司殺者殺。夫代司殺者殺,是謂代大匠斲。夫代大匠斲者,希有不傷其手矣。

74

WHEN the people are no longer afraid of death,
Why scare them with the spectre of death?

If you could make the people always afraid of death,
And they still persisted in breaking the law,
Then you might with reason arrest and execute them,
And who would dare to break the law?

Is not the Great Executor always there to kill?
To do the killing for the Great Executor
Is to chop wood for a master carpenter,
And you would be lucky indeed if you did not hurt
   your own hand!

七十五章

民之饑，以其上食稅之多，是以饑。民之難治，以其上之有爲，是以難治。民之輕死，以其求生之厚，是以輕死。夫唯無以生爲者是賢於貴生。

75

WHY are the people starving?
  Because those above them are taxing them
too heavily.
That is why they are starving.

Why are the people hard to manage?
Because those above them are fussy and have
  private ends to serve.
That is why they are hard to manage.

Why do the people make light of death?
Because those above them make too much of life.
That is why they make light of death.

The people have simply nothing to live upon!
They know better than to value such a life!

七十六章

人之生也柔弱。其死也堅強。萬物草木之生也柔脆。其死也枯槁。故堅強者死之徒。柔弱者生之徒。是以兵強則不勝。木強則兵強大處下。柔弱處上。

76

WHEN a man is living, he is soft and supple.
When he is dead, he becomes hard and rigid.
When a plant is living, it is soft and tender.
When it is dead, it becomes withered and dry.

Hence, the hard and rigid belongs to the company
of the dead:
The soft and supple belongs to the company of
the living.

Therefore, a mighty army tends to fall by its own
weight,
Just as dry wood is ready for the axe.

The mighty and great will be laid low;
The humble and weak will be exalted.

七十七章

天之道，其猶張弓與。高者抑之，下者舉之，有餘者損之，不足者補之。天道損有餘而補不足，人之道則不然。損不足以奉有餘，孰能有餘以奉天下。唯有道者，是以聖人為而不恃，功成而不處，其不欲見賢。

77

PERHAPS the Way of Heaven may be likened to the stretching of a composite bow! The upper part is depressed, while the lower is raised. If the bow-string is too long, it is cut short: if too short, it is added to.

The Way of Heaven diminishes the more-than-enough to supply the less-than-enough. The way of man is different: it takes from the less-than-enough to swell the more-than-enough. Who except a man of the Tao can put his superabundant riches to the service of the world?

Therefore, the Sage does his work without setting any store by it, accomplishes his task without dwelling upon it. He does not want his merits to be seen.

七十八章

天下莫柔弱於水。而攻堅強者莫之能勝。其無以易之。弱之勝強，柔之勝剛，天下莫不知，莫能行。是以聖人云。受國之垢，是謂社稷主，受國不祥，是謂天下王。正言若反。

78

NOTHING in the world is softer and weaker than
water;
But, for attacking the hard and strong, there is nothing
like it!
For nothing can take its place.
That the weak overcomes the strong, and the soft
overcomes the hard,
This is something known by all, but practised by none.

Therefore, the Sage says:
To receive the dirt of a country is to be the lord of
its soil-shrines.
To bear the calamities of a country is to be the prince of
the world.
Indeed, Truth sounds like its opposite!

七十九章

和大怨必有餘怨。安可以爲善是以聖人執左契而不責於人。有德司契無德司徹天道無親常與善人。

79

WHEN a great wound is healed,
  There will still remain a scar.
Can this be a desirable state of affairs?
Therefore, the Sage, holding the left-hand tally,
Performs his part of the covenant,
But lays no claims upon others.

The virtuous attends to his duties;
The virtueless knows only to levy duties upon
  the people.
The Way of Heaven has no private affections,
But always accords with the good.

八十章

小國寡民使有什伯之器而不用使民重死而不遠徙。雖有舟輿無所乘之雖有甲兵無所陳之使人復結繩而用之。甘其食美其服安其居樂其俗鄰國相望雞犬之聲相聞民至老死不相往來。

80

AH, for a small country with a small population!
Though there are highly efficient mechanical
contrivances, the people have no use for them. Let them
mind death and refrain from migrating to distant places.
Boats and carriages, weapons and armour there may still
be, but there are no occasions for using or displaying
them. Let the people revert to communication by
knotting cords. See to it that they are contented with
their food, pleased with their clothing, satisfied with
their houses, and inured to their simple ways of living.
Though there may be another country in the
neighbourhood so close that they are within sight of
each other and the crowing of cocks and barking of dogs
in one place can be heard in the other, yet there is no
traffic between them, and throughout their lives the two
peoples have nothing to do with each other.

八十一章

信言不美美言不信善者不辯辯者不善知者不博博者不知。聖人不積既以爲人已愈有既以與人已愈多。

天之道利而不害聖人之道爲而不爭。

81

SINCERE words are not sweet,
Sweet words are not sincere.
Good men are not argumentative,
The argumentative are not good.
The wise are not erudite,
The erudite are not wise.

The Sage does not take to hoarding.
The more he lives for others, the fuller is his life.
The more he gives, the more he abounds.

The Way of Heaven is to benefit, not to harm.
The Way of the Sage is to do his duty, not to strive
with anyone.

The Chinese text reproduced here is from the Lao Chieh Lao edition
compiled by Ts'ai T'ing Kan, and printed privately in 1922.
The publisher would like to thank Timothy Connor
of the Harvard–Yenching Library for his help in
locating this Chinese text & Miwako Messer
for her editorial assistance.

SHAMBHALA CLASSICS

Appreciate Your Life: The Essence of Zen Practice, by Taizan Maezumi Roshi.

The Art of Peace, by Morihei Ueshiba. Edited by John Stevens.

The Art of War, by Sun Tzu. Translated by the Denma Translation Group.

The Art of Worldly Wisdom, by Baltasar Gracián. Translated by Joseph Jacobs.

The Book of Five Rings, by Miyamoto Musashi. Translated by Thomas Cleary.

The Book of Tea, by Kakuzo Okakura.

Breath by Breath: The Liberating Practice of Insight Meditation, by Larry Rosenberg.

The Buddha and His Teachings. Edited by Samuel Bercholz and Sherab Chödzin Kohn.

The Diamond Sutra and the Sutra of Hui-Neng. Translated by Wong Mou-lam and A. F. Price.

The Eight Gates of Zen: A Program of Zen Training, by John Daido Loori.

The Great Path of Awakening, by Jamgon Kongtrul. Translated by Ken McLeod.

Insight Meditation: A Psychology of Freedom, by Joseph Goldstein.

The Japanese Art of War: Understanding the Culture of Strategy, by Thomas Cleary.

Kabbalah: The Way of the Jewish Mystic, by Perle Epstein.

Lovingkindness: The Revolutionary Art of Happiness, by Sharon Salzberg.

Meditations, by J. Krishnamurti.

Monkey: A Journey to the West, by David Kherdian.

The Myth of Freedom and the Way of Meditation, by Chögyam Trungpa.

Narrow Road to the Interior and Other Writings, by Matsuo Bashō. Translated by Sam Hamill.

The Rumi Collection: An Anthology of Translations of Mevlâna Jalâluddin Rumi. Edited by Kabir Helminski.

Seeking the Heart of Wisdom: The Path of Insight Meditation, by Joseph Goldstein and Jack Kornfield.

(Continued on next page)

Seven Taoist Masters: A Folk Novel of China. Translated by Eva Wong.

Siddhartha, by Hermann Hesse. Translated by Sherab Chödzin Kohn.

Spiritual Teaching of Ramana Maharshi, by Ramana Maharshi.

Start Where You Are: A Guide to Compassionate Living, by Pema Chödrön.

T'ai Chi Classics. Translated with commentary by Waysun Liao.

Tao Teh Ching, by Lao Tzu. Translated by John C. H. Wu.

The Taoist I Ching, by Liu I-ming. Translated by Thomas Cleary.

The Tibetan Book of the Dead: The Great Liberation through Hearing in the Bardo. Translated with commentary by Francesca Fremantle and Chögyam Trungpa.

Training the Mind and Cultivating Loving-Kindness, by Chögyam Trungpa.

The Tree of Yoga, by B. K. S. Iyengar.

The Way of the Bodhisattva, by Shantideva. Translated by the Padmakara Translation Group.

The Way of a Pilgrim and The Pilgrim Continues His Way. Translated by Olga Savin.

When Things Fall Apart: Heart Advice for Difficult Times, by Pema Chödrön.

The Wisdom of No Escape and the Path of Loving-Kindness, by Pema Chödrön.

The Wisdom of the Prophet: Sayings of Muhammad. Translated by Thomas Cleary.

The Yoga-Sūtra of Patañjali: A New Translation with Commentary. Translated by Chip Hartranft.

Zen Lessons: The Art of Leadership. Translated by Thoma Cleary.